REMEMBERING SEVEN PROPHETS

Harold B. Lee

REMEMBERING SEVEN PROPHETS

Harold B. Lee

MEMORIES OF FRANCIS M. GIBBONS
AS TOLD TO DANIEL BAY GIBBONS

Sixteen Stones Press

HOLLADAY, UTAH

Copyright © 2015 by Daniel Bay Gibbons

All rights reserved. No part of this publication may be reproduced, distributed or transmitted in any form or by any means, including photocopying, recording, or other electronic or mechanical methods, without the prior written permission of the publisher, except in the case of brief quotations embodied in critical reviews and certain other noncommercial uses permitted by copyright law.

Book layout, typography, and cover design ©2015 by Julie G. Gibbons. Photo credits: all cover photographs from the private collection of Francis M. Gibbons, used by permission. Sixteen Stones Press logo design by Marina Telezar.

Sixteen Stones Press
Publisher website: www.sixteenstonespress.com

Harold B. Lee
(Remembering Seven Prophets, Book 2)
by Daniel Bay Gibbons

Paperback ISBN 978-1-942640-13-4
eBook ISBN 978-1-942640-02-8

TABLE OF CONTENTS

Remembering Seven Prophets 1

Chronology of the Life of President Harold B. Lee 5

"The humbleness of his upbringing" 13

"Harold, stay away from that building" 15

"He earned a reputation as a brilliant young man" 16

"An aura of light surrounding the young missionary" 19

"Elder Talmage kindly pulled him aside" 20

"He visited Fern Tanner and Joan Jensen" 22

"His most distinguishing characteristic" 24

"He had a very vivid dream" 27

"He envisioned a model to help the poor" 30

"His stake patriarch was living in abject poverty" 32

"To put the priesthood quorums to work" 33

"A clear impression that he would be called" 35

"The dean of the younger men" 36

"Kid! When you're winning, don't gloat" 38

"Like a young ballplayer with his coach" 40

"The most Christlike man he had ever known" 41

"A description of the Savior" 42

"He seemed to hear a voice saying, 'Good job, boy!'" 44

"A general feeling that he would one day preside over the Church" 48

"A woman who was possessed with an evil spirit" 50

"He had a first-rate intellect and a penetrating grasp" 52

"He blessed her even as Hannah of old" 53

"This young man could fill any position in the Church" 58

"With a view to what the man may become" 60

"The most important moment of his life" 62

"A master at priesthood leadership and delegation" 64

"His daughter appeared in the sealing room" 67

"You cannot love the Lord unless you serve His people" 69

"A free interchange of ideas" 73

"Where would the Savior appear?" 75

"President Lee wrote a very gentle and
thoughtful letter" 78

"A song about President Lee" 80

"Church leaders should preach optimism,
not pessimism" 81

"He testified of the presence of spirits from
beyond the veil" 82

"They understood even before the
interpreter spoke" 83

"Experiences too sacred to discuss" 84

"He twice felt hands placed upon his head" 86

"He didn't look once at the colors" 87

"I know who your husband will be" 88

"The man the Church can least afford to
lose" 92

"The two Prophets stood upon Mars Hill as
the sun was rising" 95

"We have come to the land of miracles" 97

"A revelation that the entire church was a
single family" 101

"A dream in which he saw three men sitting
at a table" 102

"Let every man learn and act" 104

"He felt an unseen presence in the circle" 105

"President Lee could be likened to the architect" 107

"The man to lead God's people" 109

"Foxes have holes and birds have nests" 112

"One final conversation with President Lee" 113

"No righteous man dies before his time" 116

About the Author 118

Index 119

REMEMBERING SEVEN PROPHETS

This collection of reminiscences about the life of President Harold B. Lee, the eleventh President of The Church of Jesus Christ of Latter-day Saints, is part of a larger work entitled *Remembering Seven Prophets*. This work is the fruit of more than eighty hours of interviews I conducted with my father, Francis M. Gibbons, between the years 2001 to 2011, and then another dozen hours of interviews conducted between July and December of 2014 following my return from presiding over the Russia Novosibirsk Mission of the Church.

"A Plutarch to the Presidents of the Church"

Now in his ninety-fourth year, Francis M. Gibbons is perhaps the greatest student on the lives of the Presidents of the Church in this dispensation. He has two unique qualifications to speak and write about the Prophets.

First, over the past forty-five years, my father has become "a Plutarch to the Presidents of the Church." This unusual phrase has reference to Plutarch, the ancient

Greek writer, who became the most famous biographer in history, the "Father of Biography." Many years ago my father shared with my mother his special aspiration to become "a Plutarch to the Presidents of the Church, and through their lives to write the history of the Church." If any man or woman deserves the title "Plutarch to the Presidents of the Church," it is my father, Francis M. Gibbons. Over the past four decades he has become by far the most prolific writer of biographies of the Presidents of the Church, writing a full-length biography of every Prophet from Joseph Smith to Gordon B. Hinckley. Dad's biographies of the Prophets have been very popular, selling many hundreds of thousands of copies. Thirteen of his presidential biographies have been included in Brigham Young University's list of "Sixty Significant Mormon Biographies." He has truly become "a Plutarch to the Presidents of the Church."

"A Scribe to the Prophets"

Second, my father has been a personal witness and observer of the character of the last seven Presidents of the Church: Presidents Joseph Fielding Smith, Harold B.

Lee, Spencer W. Kimball, Ezra Taft Benson, Howard W. Hunter, Gordon B. Hinckley, and Thomas S. Monson. He knew these men personally. He worked with them. While serving from 1970 to 1986 as the secretary to the First Presidency and later as a member of the Seventy, Dad associated with them on a daily basis. He was a "Scribe to the Prophets," as were William Clayton, Wilford Woodruff, Joseph F. Smith, William F. Gibbons, Joseph Anderson, and others before him.

"I am their witness"

When Dad was sustained as a General Authority in April of 1986, after many years serving as the faithful scribe for the Presidents of the Church, he said:

> The Church is led by prophets, seers and revelators. I am their witness. I testify that they are honorable, upright, dedicated men of integrity, committed to teaching the principles of the gospel, who strive with all of their might to prepare a people ready for the return of the head of the Church, Jesus Christ, at His second coming.

REMEMBERING SEVEN PROPHETS

This work, *Remembering Seven Prophets*, shares many unique stories, anecdotes, insights, and testimonies about the last seven Presidents of the Church, which are nowhere else available.

I offer this work for the enlightenment and inspiration of the reader and as a tribute to the memory of the seven Presidents of the Church featured in these pages. I love and honor these great men and add my witness to that of my father that they were and are Prophets of God!

Daniel Bay Gibbons
February 5, 2015
Holladay, Utah

CHRONOLOGY OF THE LIFE OF PRESIDENT HAROLD B. LEE

March 28, 1899
Harold Bingham Lee is born in Clifton, Idaho, to Samuel Marion Lee, Jr., and Louisa Bingham.

1916
Harold B. Lee moves away from home to attend the Albion State Normal School, where he obtains a secondary teaching certificate.

1916
Harold B. Lee teaches grammar school in Weston, Idaho.

1917
Harold B. Lee is hired as the principal of a grammar school in Oxford, Idaho, at the age of eighteen. He continues in Oxford for three years.

September 1920
Harold B. Lee is called to serve in the Western States Mission.

December 1922
Harold B. Lee completes his mission and returns home.

December 22, 1922
Following his mission, Harold B. Lee speaks at the Ensign Stake conference with Church President Heber J. Grant in attendance.

November 14, 1923
Harold B. Lee is married to Fern Tanner in the Salt Lake Temple.

October 1928
Harold B. Lee is sustained, without prior notice, as a counselor in the Pioneer Stake presidency.

October 1930
Harold B. Lee is called and sustained as president of the Pioneer Stake. At age thirty-one, he is the youngest stake president in the Church at the time.

December 1, 1932
Harold B. Lee is sworn in as a Salt Lake City Commissioner.

1933
Harold B. Lee is reelected to a full term on the Salt Lake City Commission.

April 30, 1935
Harold B. Lee meets with Presidents Heber J. Grant and David O. McKay to brief them on the welfare initiatives he created in the Pioneer Stake.

June 1, 1935
Harold B. Lee presents a general plan to the First Presidency for implementing a Church-wide welfare model.

April 10, 1941
Harold B. Lee is sustained as a member of the Quorum of the Twelve Apostles.

1942
Elder Harold B. Lee accompanies President J. Reuben Clark to attend Church meetings in Arizona. While speaking in a stake conference in Safford, Arizona, President Clark tells the saints that it is likely that Elder Harold B. Lee will one day become the President of the Church.

1944
Elder Harold B. Lee and his wife and daughters spend five weeks traveling in Mexico.

1945
Elder Harold B. Lee gives several radio talks that are later compiled into a book titled, *Youth and the Church.*

1947
Elder Harold B. Lee accompanies Elder Charles A. Callis to create the first stake in the Southern States, in Jacksonville, Florida. He then presides at funeral services for Elder Callis, who dies the day following the stake creation..

1948
During a single week, Elder Harold B. Lee performs twenty-three temple marriages.

March 11, 1956
Elder Harold B. Lee has a special spiritual experience during the dedication of the Los Angeles Temple.

1958
Elder Harold B. Lee and his wife, Fern, tour the South Africa Mission, followed by a three-month tour of South America.

September 24, 1962
President Harold B. Lee's first wife, Fern Tanner Lee, passes away.

June 17, 1963
Elder Harold B. Lee is sealed to his second wife, Joan Jensen Lee, in the Salt Lake Temple.

January 18, 1970
President David O. McKay dies. Elder Harold B. Lee is called as first counselor to President McKay's successor, President Joseph Fielding Smith.

February 1970
President Harold B. Lee convenes a meeting in New York City focused on taking the initiative in media coverage regarding the Church. Included in the meeting are high leaders of the Church and LDS leaders in business and the professions.

August 1971
President Harold B. Lee joins President Joseph Fielding Smith and seven members of the Twelve in attending the first area general conference of the Church, held in Manchester, England.

July 2, 1972
President Joseph Fielding Smith passes away.

July 7, 1972
President Harold B. Lee is ordained and set apart as the eleventh President of the Church.

August 1972
President Harold B. Lee travels to Mexico to preside at the area conference in Mexico City.

September 1972
President Harold B. Lee and Elder Gordon B. Hinckley of the Twelve travel throughout Europe and the Middle East. President Lee's life is miraculously preserved in Jerusalem.

August 1973
President Harold B. Lee heads a delegation from Church headquarters to attend the area conference in Munich, Germany.

December 26, 1973
President Harold B. Lee dies suddenly during a routine medical checkup.

"The Humbleness of His Upbringing"

Many of the great qualities President Harold B. Lee possessed in the years of his great service were acquired as a young farm boy. President Lee was born in the most humble of circumstances, and throughout his life he reflected the humbleness of his upbringing. He was born and raised in Clifton, Idaho, which is a very small farming community in the extreme northern end of the Cache Valley. His ancestors were largely Scottish and Irish, and his people were hardworking.

There was never much money in the Lee household, but he had a remarkable mother, Louisa Lee, who made sure that Harold was raised in a home of culture and refinement. Harold was taught to play the piano as a very young boy and played throughout his life. He also played the trombone, and—like one of his successors, President Howard W. Hunter—he played in a dance band as a young man. In later years, President Lee was often called upon to play the piano or organ in meetings of the First Presidency and the Quorum of the Twelve.

"HAROLD, STAY AWAY FROM THAT BUILDING"

Even as a little boy, President Lee developed a powerful spirituality. I heard him several times relate this story from his early childhood: When he was a very little boy living in Clifton, Idaho, he started to walk one day toward an old abandoned barn or outbuilding on his father's farm. He said that the building had not been used for many years and was in serious disrepair, with the roof beginning to cave in. As he walked toward the building, President Lee said that he heard an audible voice. The voice said: "Harold, stay away from that building!" He looked around, expecting to see his father or one of the neighboring farmers nearby, but found no one. He heeded that warning voice and stayed away from the building. He never knew what danger might have been lurking in the old building, but he learned at a very tender age to recognize and follow the voice of the Spirit.

In my view, this became the prime motivating force in his life—to hear and heed the voice of the Spirit.

"HE EARNED A REPUTATION AS A BRILLIANT YOUNG MAN"

President Harold B. Lee acquired his early education in the grammar school in his tiny hometown of Clifton and then later at the Oneida Stake Academy in Preston, Idaho. In those days there was no government-sponsored education beyond the grammar school grades, and so the Church stepped in to create stake academies. The academies taught all the standard curriculum of a contemporary high school and prepared their students for college or for work in the trades. They also provided religious education.

President Lee was at the stake academy for four years, where he earned a reputation as a brilliant young man. He was a remarkable young man, by all accounts: a top scholar, a student body leader, an athlete, a debater, a writer for the school newspaper, and a musician. Even at that tender age he was what you may call a Renaissance man.

One of the long-lasting friendships President Lee formed at the stake academy in Preston was with future Church President Ezra Taft Benson, who was from another tiny

Mormon farming town located not far from Clifton. President Benson was only a few months younger than President Lee, and they became close friends. I find it quite remarkable that two contemporary farm boys from tiny villages in the same remote valley would both live to serve for decades together in the Quorum of the Twelve and then both preside over the Church. It says something for the Cache Valley—and for the many, many other scattered Mormon communities from Canada to Mexico—that it would produce two boys who would grow into men of such stature.

At age seventeen President Lee was admitted to the Albion State School. Albion was two hundred miles from Cache Valley, and President Lee boarded with a Mormon family. It was essentially the first time in his life that he had associated with nonmembers of the Church.

After one semester in Albion, President Lee obtained a teaching certificate, qualifying him to teach grammar school. He soon was hired at age seventeen to teach in Weston, Idaho, a few miles from his hometown of Clifton. On weekends he rode home to Clifton on his horse, where he attended church with his family, and then each Monday morning rode the horse back to Weston.

The following year, President Lee was hired as the principal of a school in Oxford, another little Mormon farming town north of Clifton. He was only eighteen years old, and he had two other teachers working under him. Again, President Lee rode his horse home every weekend to stay with his family in Clifton, where he served as the elders' quorum president in the Clifton Ward.

"AN AURA OF LIGHT SURROUNDING THE YOUNG MISSIONARY"

Beginning in 1920, President Lee served a full-time mission in the Western States Mission. The mission headquarters were in Denver, where President Lee spent much of his mission serving as a conference president in the largest conference in the mission.

I heard the following story from several sources, and its accuracy was later confirmed to me by President Lee: One of the stalwart members of the Church in Denver, a Sister Harriet Jensen, had a remarkable spiritual experience during the time of President Lee's service there. She said that once during a meeting in Denver when young Elder Harold B. Lee spoke, she saw an aura of light surrounding the young missionary as he stood at the pulpit. After the meeting, this sister sought out President Lee and told him, with great emotion, "Someday you will be the President of the Church!"

"Elder Talmage kindly pulled him aside"

President Lee once shared with me this experience he had during his mission to Colorado, which provided crucial leadership lessons for the young man: During the time when President Lee served as the conference president, he once conducted a baptismal service. As President Lee stood at the pulpit, about to start the meeting, his mission president, John M. Knight, and a visiting Apostle, Elder James E. Talmage, walked unexpectedly into the chapel. The visiting leaders came forward and took seats on the stand. President Lee, who was still standing at the pulpit, was somewhat surprised and mildly flustered, and he immediately began the meeting without recognizing the visiting authorities or first conferring with them, as standard church protocol would dictate.

The meeting proceeded. Several new converts received the ordinance of baptism. As the baptisms were about to proceed, Elder Talmage, the visiting Apostle, suddenly stepped forward to the edge of the font and stood there, carefully watching what went on.

Then, after the baptisms, when the confirmations began, Elder Talmage again stepped forward uninvited and said to Harold B. Lee, "Here, young man. I'll confirm this one." President Lee told me that in performing the confirmation, Elder Talmage deliberately reversed the customary order and first said, "Receive ye the Holy Ghost," and then afterward he confirmed the candidate a member of the Church.

After the meeting, Elder Talmage kindly took pulled President Lee aside, put his arm around his shoulder and told him that he had done a marvelous job conducting. Then, having built the young man up, he proceeded to instruct him in priesthood governance. He pointed out the young missionary's error in failing to recognize the presiding authority and checking with him before he proceeded. He also emphasized that there is no set wording to confirm someone a member of the Church.

President Lee told me that this kind but direct tutoring from one of the Apostles was one of the most important leadership lessons he ever learned.

"HE VISITED FERN TANNER AND JOAN JENSEN"

During President Lee's mission, he met several people who would play important roles in his future life. One of these was Elder James E. Talmage, who carried to the leading councils a good report of the young missionary from Cache Valley. Another important person in his future life was his mission president, John M. Knight, who opened many doors for his young missionary as President Lee began his post-mission life. Other important connections were made with his fellow missionaries. Two others I might mention who played key future roles in President Lee's life were a full-time missionary, Sister Fern Tanner, who had served under his leadership in Denver, and Joan Jensen, a beautiful young woman who was the girlfriend of one of his missionary companions.

President Lee completed his mission at the end of 1922 and traveled first to Salt Lake City, where his mission president had arranged for the young returned missionary to speak in a stake conference in the Ensign Stake. Attending the conference was Church

President Heber J. Grant and several other General Authorities. I'm sure that this was a heady and likely an intimidating experience for a farm boy from Idaho—to preach a sermon with the President of the Church seated behind him!

After the conference, President Lee had plans to travel home to Clifton to be reunited with his family for the first time in two years. Before leaving Salt Lake City, however, he visited Sister Tanner and Sister Jensen in their homes, as well as several former missionary companions.

I have always thought that it is an intriguing coincidence that these two young women, Sister Fern Tanner and Sister Joan Jensen, were both destined to marry President Lee. Sister Fern Tanner, of course, became President Lee's wife less than a year after he was released from his mission. They carried on a long-distance courtship between Cache Valley and Salt Lake City. Joan Jensen, who was dating President Lee's former missionary companion, later broke up with the young man, and she remained single for many decades until she became the Prophet's second wife, after the death of Sister Fern Tanner Lee.

"His most distinguishing characteristic"

I once heard President Lee say that he never had any specific plans in his life other than to follow the dictates of the Spirit wherever they might lead. That is the kind of life-philosophy that might have been followed by Nephi himself. Throughout his life, President Lee listened for the voice of the Spirit and then acted upon the promptings he received. He was a very spiritually sensitive man, perhaps more so than any other man I have ever known. Spirituality, in my mind, was his most distinguishing characteristic.

This habit of listening to the Spirit and then immediately acting was the pattern President Lee followed upon returning home from the Western States Mission. He was not ambitious in a worldly sense, but he was extraordinarily prayerful and diligent. Those early post-mission years were crucial for President Lee. Within only a decade following his mission he had become a well-known, substantial, trusted, and gifted man. But the stature he achieved in that first post-mission decade was not the result of a deliberate program of pursuing a specific set of worldly goals. Rather, President Lee simply followed the Spirit, and the result was that he had, as Shakespeare said, "greatness thrust upon him."

After his marriage to Fern Tanner, the young couple rented a tiny house in the Poplar Grove Ward of the Pioneer Stake, while President Lee taught at the Whittier Elementary School. A short time later, President Lee was sought out and hired as a manager of the Foundation Press. With increased prosperity, the Lees bought a home, also in the Pioneer Stake. President Lee fulfilled a string of significant church callings, including on the stake high council. Then in 1928, only six years after returning from his mission, President Lee was sustained as a counselor in the stake presidency. He was given no advance notice of his call before the stake conference meeting in which he was sustained. President Lee learned of his new calling along with the rest of the stake when the presiding authority read his name! He was only twenty-nine years old at the time. Two years later he was called as the president of the Pioneer Stake, and for some time he was the youngest stake president in the Church.

A short time after his call as stake president, his former mission president, John M. Knight, called President Lee with an interesting and intriguing question. Would President Lee consider an appointment to the Salt Lake City Commission to fill a vacancy caused by the death of another commissioner? President Knight at the time was filling another seat as a Commissioner. President Lee counseled with his wife and prayed about it. The Spirit dictated that he accept, and he did so. He was installed in office in 1935 and a few months later was reelected to a full term. He served in this role until 1935, when he went to work for the Church as the managing director of the Church's new Welfare Department.

His two roles as stake president in one of the largest stakes in the Church and as a city commissioner vaulted President Lee into the spotlight. Without ever setting about on a path to achieve public notoriety, the Spirit had led him into positions of high influence as a very young man.

"He had a very vivid dream"

President Lee shared with me a significant spiritual experience he had in connection with his call to serve as a stake president at age thirty-one: The Friday before the reorganization of the stake, he received a surprise telephone call asking him to go to the Church Administration building for an interview. President Lee said that he hurried over to 47 East South Temple and was invited into the office of President Rudger Clawson, the President of the Quorum of the Twelve. President Lee was surprised to find a second Apostle, Elder George Albert Smith, sitting in the room. Elder Smith was second in seniority in the Quorum behind President Clawson. Elder George Albert Smith, of course, was destined to become the next President of the Church in a very few years following the death of President Heber J. Grant.

In President Clawson's office, Harold B. Lee was quickly informed that he had been chosen by the First Presidency and the Quorum of the Twelve to be the new president of the Pioneer Stake. President Lee said that this call shocked him to the core, as he was only thirty-one years old at the time. He began to tell the Apostles that he would much prefer working as a counselor to one of the older, experienced brethren in the stake. President Lee told me that Elder George Albert Smith interrupted him and told him very directly that they hadn't invited him in to ask him what should be done, but rather to learn what the Lord wanted him to do. President Lee accepted the call and then asked the two Apostles if they had any suggestions about his counselors. President Lee was again surprised by the response. They told him that they had two specific brethren in mind, but that they weren't going to tell him who they were. They suggested that he pray about it. Elder George Albert Smith told him, "If you are led by the Spirit of the Lord, you will choose the two men whom we have in mind." He was instructed to present the names of his counselors the next morning.

President Lee told me that he was very shaken by this interview and with the prospect of assuming such a heavy priesthood responsibility. He pondered the question of his counselors throughout the rest of the day and evening. During the evening he tentatively chose two men to nominate as counselors.

Before retiring to bed for the night he knelt down and prayed with great fervency, but still went to bed in a very agitated state of mind. He said that after falling into a fitful sleep, he had a very vivid dream. In his dream, he commenced his service as stake president with the two counselors he had tentatively chosen. It seemed he was trying to hold presidency and council meetings with them, but misunderstandings and disagreements arose and multiplied, and President Lee awoke from his dream realizing that his first choices were wrong. He lay awake in his bed pondering other alternatives, then fell back asleep. Again, he had a dream in which obstacles and bad feelings arose, and he again awoke. He said that this process went on several times throughout the night, and by morning he felt he was certain whom the Lord wanted to serve in the stake presidency.

Later that day, he met with President Rudger Clawson and Elder George Albert Smith and gave to them the names of two men. The two senior Apostles then told President Lee that these were the two counselors they had in mind all along.

"He Envisioned a Model to Help the Poor"

President Harold B. Lee served as a stake president in the Pioneer Stake during the onset of the Great Depression. The Pioneer Stake included many of Salt Lake City's poorest neighborhoods, and the membership was hard hit economically. More than half of the membership of the stake was out of work and reliant upon outside help. Even as a young man, President Lee was a true visionary, and he envisioned a model to help the poor and unemployed in his stake. Rather than simply giving needy members a dole, President Lee taught that members should be expected to work or give service for food or other help they received from the Church. President Lee realized that the idle manpower among his priesthood brethren was a great reservoir upon which the stake could draw. The stake owned a farm, and President Lee put the brethren to work helping with the harvest in exchange for a share of the crops. All the surplus food not divided among the families of the farm workers was canned. The stake bought a warehouse where they made furniture, clothing, and bedding. This warehouse became known as the "storehouse." President Lee devised a system whereby his bishops could make "withdrawals" from the storehouse for their needy members. President Lee also put unemployed brethren to work building a stake gymnasium, which was used for athletic and cultural events. It became the center of Church life in the Pioneer Stake. These far-seeing efforts to lift the people economically received great attention in the Church and in the nation. And behind this great attention was the young visionary leader who had been the architect: Harold B. Lee.

"HIS STAKE PATRIARCH WAS LIVING IN ABJECT POVERTY"

Elder Theodore M. Burton, a long-time General Authority who was raised in the Pioneer Stake during the time President Lee was the stake president, shared with me some of the human background of the creation of the Church welfare program. He told me that early in his service leading the stake, President Lee made the shocking discovery that his stake patriarch was living in abject poverty—without work, income, savings, or even food to put on his table. President Lee immediately gave the patriarch temporal assistance and then began to see to the needs of thousands of other stake members. From this humble beginning sprang the vast, worldwide Church welfare program.

"To Put the Priesthood Quorums to Work"

On April 30, 1935, President Lee was invited to meet with the First Presidency to explain the welfare initiatives he had created in the Pioneer Stake. The result was that President Lee was asked by President Heber J. Grant to write a proposal whereby the model of welfare assistance he had built in the Pioneer Stake could be extended to the entire Church. He did so, and a year later, on April 15, 1936, the First Presidency called President Lee to head up a new Church Welfare Department. This was a full-time endeavor, and it necessitated his release as stake president and his resignation from the Salt Lake City Commission. From that date until his death, President Lee was engaged in full-time service for the Church.

President Lee shared with me a special spiritual experience he had after receiving the assignment from President Grant to draw up a general plan for the entire Church to implement the initiatives he had created in the Pioneer Stake. After meeting with the First Presidency and receiving his assignment on

April 30, President Lee said that he drove up into City Creek Canyon, near downtown Salt Lake City, and walked into a secluded stand of trees, where he knelt down and sought for divine guidance. He said that a great peace came over him, together with this insight: there was no need to create any new organization to care for the poor and the needy, but only to put the priesthood quorums to work.

"A CLEAR IMPRESSION THAT HE WOULD BE CALLED"

President Lee told me of a special experience he had in connection with his call to serve in the Quorum of the Twelve. A few days before he was sustained, he arose from his bed in the morning and received a clear impression that he would be called as a member of the Quorum of the Twelve. He said that the impression was definite and unmistakable. He pondered the impression throughout the day as he went about his work. That evening he received a message to go to the office of President Heber J. Grant, then the President of the Church, where he was called to the apostleship.

"THE DEAN OF THE YOUNGER MEN"

It is clear to me that President J. Reuben Clark exerted an unusually strong influence over President Harold B. Lee, as he did over many other General Authorities. In a sense, President Lee idolized President J. Reuben Clark, as did most of those who worked closely with him—there was a certain awe and almost a reverence toward President Clark. I saw this great respect for President Clark's memory mirrored in most of the leading Brethren of the Church.

When President Lee was called to the Twelve in 1941, he was a very young man in a Quorum filled with old soldiers, and President Clark took him under his wing, so to speak, to school him in his new and sacred calling. Soon after President Lee's call to the Twelve, several of the senior Brethren passed away, and then many other young men were called to the apostleship. These included Elders Spencer W. Kimball, Ezra Taft Benson, Mark E. Petersen, Matthew Cowley, Henry D. Moyle, Delbert L. Stapley, and Marion G. Romney. Because of the contrasting youth of these men, President J. Reuben Clark was fond of referring to them as "the younger men," and he called President Lee, "The dean of the younger men."

President Clark also began to call him "Kid." This was not a sign of disrespect toward the young Apostle. To the contrary, it was a sign of great affection for the aged Apostle to speak to his young Quorum member in this manner. He apparently did the same with most of the other younger Brethren. He did this only in private settings and in a loving manner. For example, President Lee told me that in the early years of the implementation of the Church welfare program, when there was much opposition by many Church leaders, President Clark came to him and said, "Never mind, Kid. Just stay with it and some day they will all want to climb on the bandwagon."

"KID! WHEN YOU'RE WINNING, DON'T GLOAT"

During the years President Lee served as a counselor to President Joseph Fielding Smith, he once told me this fascinating story involving President J. Reuben Clark: As previously mentioned, before his call as a General Authority, President Lee was employed by the Church as the director of the Church's newly implemented welfare program. At the time, President Lee was a very young man with a great deal of responsibility. He was also a Church employee, not an ecclesiastical leader, as were the General Authorities. Because President Lee had pioneered the principles of Church welfare in the stake over which he presided, he knew what he was doing, but he occasionally had differences of opinion with some of the long-time Church employees. On one occasion, President Lee told me, he had a difference of opinion about the welfare program with one of the General Authorities, a man of great Church experience who was much older than President Lee. President Lee respectfully deferred to this man, because he outranked him in authority, but President Lee still considered himself to be in the right. A short time later, President Lee was called to the Quorum of the Twelve, and suddenly he outranked this General Authority. One day, not long after his new call, President Lee was visiting with President Clark, and he made the comment, "Now that I am a member of the Twelve, perhaps this General Authority will pay some attention to me." President Lee said that President Clark was silent and considered this for a few moments, then told President Lee: "Let me give you some advice, Kid. When you're winning, don't gloat." In other words, even though he now outranked this General Authority, he should show him the courtesy and kindness that this person had failed to show to President Lee.

"Like a Young Ballplayer with His Coach"

Like President J. Reuben Clark before him, President Lee exerted an unusually strong influence over those with whom he worked closely. There was a quality in his personality that seemed to impel others to want to please him. President Boyd K. Packer once told me that when he was around President Lee he always felt like a young ballplayer with his coach. President Lee was the best of mentors. He was inspiring, but tough. He knew from personal experience what he was talking about. Like young athletes around their coach, everyone wanted to please President Lee. To hear President Lee say, "Well done!" was among the highest of accolades.

"THE MOST CHRISTLIKE MAN HE HAD EVER KNOWN"

I have already alluded to the special relationship that existed between President Lee and President J. Reuben Clark. President Clark was a great mentor for President Lee, especially in his early years of service in the Quorum of the Twelve. President Lee also spoke often of a second exemplar that affected his life greatly. This was Elder Nicholas G. Smith, who served as an Acting Patriarch to the Church from 1932 to 1934, and then as an Assistant to the Quorum of the Twelve from 1941 to 1945. President Harold B. Lee once told me that Nicholas G. Smith was the most Christlike man he had ever known. President Lee and Elder Smith occupied offices side by side in the Church Administration Building for many years. He told me that they agreed at the beginning that the door connecting the two offices would never be locked. This was emblematic of their relationship, as well. There was never any barrier between the two.

"A DESCRIPTION OF THE SAVIOR"

President Lee had a picture in his office of the Savior, which was given to him by Elder Samuel O. Bennion in 1945, shortly before Elder Bennion's death. President Lee first showed me this picture in 1970, when he asked me to visit with him in his office. Elder Bennion had served for many years as a member of the First Council of the Seventy. President Lee told me that this picture was the most accurate representation he had ever seen, based upon a description of the Savior given by Elder Orson F. Whitney, who saw the Savior in the Salt Lake Temple. President Lee told me that this was the picture that Orson F. Whitney had selected as best depicting the appearance and character of the Savior. President Lee said that based upon Elder Whitney's description and testimony and "other things," he knew that the representations we often see of the Savior are not accurate.

On a later occasion when I was in President Lee's office, after he became President of the Church, he referred again to this same picture of the Savior. He told me that it reflected a character of love, with firmness and strength—a leader capable of driving the moneychangers out of the temple, yet kind and loving enough to hold and bless a little child.

On still another occasion, President Lee told me this story: He said that early in his service as an Apostle, he was traveling with Elder Charles A. Callis of the Twelve. He said that Elder Callis began to tell President Lee of an occasion when the Savior had appeared to him, and they were interrupted, and he was never privileged to hear the account in its entirety, which was a great sadness to President Lee.

"HE SEEMED TO HEAR A VOICE SAYING, 'GOOD JOB, BOY!'"

President Lee was called to the Twelve in April of 1941. In January of 1947, while he was still a very junior member of the Quorum of the Twelve, he had one of the most difficult yet spiritually significant experiences of his life to that point. He later shared this experience with me in some detail: President Lee was assigned to assist in the creation of a new stake in Jacksonville, Florida—the first stake of the Church in the Southern States—as the junior companion to one of the senior Apostles, Elder Charles A. Callis. Elder Callis had previously served as a mission president in the South, and was well known and much beloved of the people. When the conference was over, Elder Callis went to President Lee and said with a twinkle in his eye, "Harold, I surely want to thank you for your help, especially because you didn't cross me."

After the conference, Brother Callis insisted that President Lee drive down to Miami with the mission president, Heber Meeks. Brother Callis then said to President Lee grandly, "I want you to see my country as it really is." President Lee and the mission president set out in the car and had traveled some distance through central and southern Florida, when they were stopped by a highway patrolman. The officer informed them that the police had been searching for them all up and down the length of the highway and that there was a "death notice" waiting for their phone call in Jacksonville. They immediately called back to Jacksonville. It was regarding Brother Callis. He had died suddenly back in Jacksonville the day after the creation of the stake.

President Lee was directed by the First Presidency to hold the funeral there in Jacksonville, rather than transport Elder Callis's body back to Salt Lake City. Because of the long distance, none of the other General Authorities attended the funeral, and President Lee had to handle it alone. President Lee told me that this was one of the most difficult experiences he has ever had, particularly because of his closeness to Elder Callis.

The funeral services were held the following Thursday. At the funeral service, President Lee received a telegram from the First Presidency, which they asked be read to the congregation. President Lee said that as he read it, he was instantly filled with such an overwhelming emotion that he couldn't speak, and so he asked President Meeks, the mission president, to read it to the congregation for him. President Lee said that he had seldom felt so alone and oppressed.

Then President Lee told me that later during the service, he suddenly felt a great lifting of the clouds, as it were. A great calm, a great peace, descended upon him. He was flooded by a great feeling of peace and well-being. From that moment forward, he was greatly buoyed up and seemed unusually filled with the Spirit as he concluded the funeral service.

President Lee told me that following the funeral services, he went into a room in the Church house alone to collect his hat and coat. As he entered the room, he seemed to hear the audible voice of Charles A. Callis saying, "Good job, boy!"

When President Lee returned to Salt Lake City, he visited with President Stephen L. Richards, a counselor in the First Presidency. President Richards told President Lee that the Brethren had been thinking of him during the difficult experiences of the past week.

Remembering how he had felt unusually buoyed up during Elder Callis's funeral service, President Lee asked President Richards if anything unusual had occurred during the Thursday council meeting of the First Presidency and the Twelve. "Why yes," President Richards said. "President McKay offered a special prayer for you and implored the Lord especially in your behalf. And we all felt a great peace." President Lee told me that as far as he can calculate it, he felt a calm descend upon him in Jacksonville at the precise moment the Prophet and Apostles were praying for him back in Salt Lake City.

President Lee told me that this was one of the most dramatic illustrations of the great power of prayer he had ever experienced.

"A GENERAL FEELING THAT HE WOULD ONE DAY PRESIDE OVER THE CHURCH"

President Harold B. Lee was sustained as a member of the Quorum of the Twelve in April of 1941, when he had just turned forty-two years of age. At the time of his call, he was the youngest Apostle by many years and most of his brethren in the Quorum were senior to him by three, four, or five decades.

Because of President Lee's youth, there was a perception in the Church from the very moment of his call that he would serve as the President of the Church one day. This feeling was shared by the highest leadership of the Church. For example, about a year after his call to the Twelve, President Lee accompanied a member of the First Presidency, President J. Reuben Clark, to a stake conference in Safford, Arizona. This, incidentally, was the stake that future Apostle and future Church President Spencer W. Kimball presided over. While speaking in the general session of the stake conference, President Clark told the assembled saints that it was likely that Elder

Harold B. Lee would one day become President of the Church.

I am certain that President Lee felt uncomfortable with these kinds of public expressions about his future. He was an innately humble man who did not go out of his way to seek the spotlight. At the same time, I am confident that President Lee himself had a sense of what was to come in his life.

"A WOMAN WHO WAS POSSESSED WITH AN EVIL SPIRIT"

The following significant story was told to me by my friend, Oscar W. McConkie, Jr., and later corroborated by President Harold B. Lee himself: In 1949 President Lee toured the California Mission with the mission president, Oscar W. McConkie, Sr. Member meetings were held throughout the mission, and President Lee traveled by car with the mission president. As the two of them were driving through Death Valley, the lowest point in North America at nearly 300 feet below sea level, President McConkie shared a vivid dream he had received in which Satan had appeared to him. After pondering this for some time in the car, President Lee offered a private interpretation of the dream. He then told President McConkie about an experience he had with a woman who was possessed with an evil spirit, who said to him, "You are the head of the Church!" In response to this, President McConkie told President Lee that perhaps the evil spirit in the woman had spoken not of the present, but of the future. The implication was that even the evil adversary knew what Harold

B. Lee was destined to become during his lifetime.

"HE HAD A FIRST-RATE INTELLECT AND A PENETRATING GRASP"

My first acquaintance with President Harold B. Lee occurred in the late 1940's while I was studying at Stanford University in California. From the outset I was impressed with President Lee's mental powers. He had a first-rate intellect and a penetrating grasp, not only of scripture and doctrine, but also of history, literature, and current world events.

He also had a phenomenal memory. This was illustrated immediately after I began working as the secretary to the First Presidency in 1970. When President Lee first greeted me as I commenced my service, he extended his hand and said, "Brother Gibbons, we met first in Palo Alto, didn't we?" Though it had been nearly twenty-five years since I had first met him, he remembered me. I thought this remarkable, considering the many thousands and tens of thousands of saints President Lee had met during his thirty years of membership in the Quorum of the Twelve.

"HE BLESSED HER EVEN AS HANNAH OF OLD"

As I mentioned, I first met President Harold B. Lee in 1948. My wife, Helen, and I were living in Palo Alto, California, while I was attending law school at Stanford University. We belonged to a study group that included President Lee's daughter, Maurine, and her husband, Ernie Wilkins, who was also a Stanford student. Usually, when President Lee had a conference assignment in the Northern California area, Ernie and Maurine would arrange a meeting of the study group in their home, where we were privileged to receive counsel and instruction from President Lee, then an Apostle, in an intimate, relaxed setting.

At the time, Helen and I were childless, although we had been married for some time. In our patriarchal blessings, we had each been promised both sons and daughters, and so we were very anxious to have a family. But after five years of marriage, we had been unable to conceive.

In early 1950, during one of Elder Lee's visits to Palo Alto, Helen felt inspired to seek a blessing from him. In it, he blessed her that the vital functions of her body would be quickened by the Holy Spirit to begin the processes that would result in motherhood, and he specifically blessed her, "even as Hannah of old," and counseled her to covenant with the Lord in her secret prayers as Hannah had done. He also blessed her with peace of mind and faith, and that if there should be a space of time before she conceived, we should spend that time in service to the Church, in opening our hearts to other children, and proving ourselves worthy of parenthood. He also conferred a special blessing on the doctors who would serve her, that they would be especially inspired in exercising their medical skills in Helen's behalf.

We endeavored, as best we could, to comply with all the conditions Elder Lee had mentioned. We were active in our ward in Palo Alto, filling assignments in Relief Society and Sunday School. We did babysitting for our friends, took Helen's young brother into our home, and even applied to adopt a baby through the California placement service. As far as we can determine, Helen conceived about the time of our visit to the California state agency in San Francisco.

Everything went well with the pregnancy until about three weeks before the expected delivery, when Helen developed a severe pain in her side. The doctor thought her complaints were merely the reaction of a woman pregnant for the first time who did not realize what to expect in carrying a child. Nevertheless, after the complaints continued, he hospitalized Helen to conduct tests, which revealed nothing.

The evening before the baby's birth, the doctor visited Helen in the hospital again and, finding no clues to the root of her trouble, went home. He later told us that he became uneasy as he thought about Helen, and that he felt compelled to return to the hospital. When he arrived and examined her again, he discovered that the baby was in distress, which caused him to decide immediately on a Caesarean section. The doctor contacted me at home to obtain my consent. I barely had time to arrange for a neighbor, Mac Van Valkenburg, to accompany me to the hospital, where we administered to Helen.

After the doctor had taken the baby, he discovered the root of Helen's pain. Somehow, circulation had been cut off to one ovary, resulting in a strangulated ovary. By that time, the lack of circulation had caused the ovary and all the surrounding tissue to become gangrenous, requiring its removal. Had he induced labor as he had thought to do earlier in the evening, or had there been a delay of as much as a half hour in taking the baby, it is almost certain that Suzanne would have been born dead or with serious brain damage because of the lack of oxygen, and Helen would have lost her life.

After the delivery, a nurse told Helen that someone should go to church the next day, Sunday, and thank God that she and the baby were alive and well, which I did, as it was fast Sunday.

A few months after the birth, I wrote President Lee a letter, detailing the circumstances of Suzanne's miraculous birth and of the unusual way in which his blessing to Helen had been fulfilled.

Many years later, and shortly after I began my service to the First Presidency, President Lee came to my office one morning. He said that he had been looking through his "miracle file" and found the letter I had written to him almost twenty years before, telling about

Helen's blessing and Suzanne's birth. He asked about Suzanne then, as he often did thereafter; and when she was sealed to Timothy A. Burton in February of 1972 in the Salt Lake Temple, President Lee graciously performed the sealing.

The day before President Lee's death, he called me at home to wish me and my family a Merry Christmas. Almost the last words I ever heard him speak in mortality were to ask, "How is our miracle girl?"

I understand that experiences of this kind were repeated time and again during President Lee's ministry. He was and is a true prophet of God, richly endowed with spiritual perceptions and sensitivities possessed by few of God's servants.

"THIS YOUNG MAN COULD FILL ANY POSITION IN THE CHURCH"

Like a coach who works to develop his best players, President Harold B. Lee was constantly aware of the need to train up future leaders of the Church. He would often inquire about the progress of promising young Church leaders in Europe, the Pacific, or Latin America. Perhaps because he had been tapped for high Church leadership at such a young age, he seemed to show a special interest in young leaders who were thrust into significant Church callings at a young age, and he went out of his way to teach them and to help them.

One day a young stake president came in to visit with President Lee when he served as President of the Church. The young man's name was David Stanley, and he was probably the youngest stake president in the Church at the time. He was in his early thirties and presided over the Pioneer Stake, the same stake President Lee had presided over when he was a young man. President Stanley told the Prophet that his stake was suffering greatly because of the loss of the old neighborhoods to industrial development and the new freeway system. The new freeway had bisected his stake, isolating several old neighborhoods. He told President Lee that he was trying to help attract stable families to come live in the Pioneer Stake and wanted the Church to consider buying some abandoned schools, to subdivide them and sell the lots as residential home sites. This would help provide an atmosphere attractive to families, the young stake president said. President Lee listened to this young man with great respect and then granted his request. After President Stanley left the room, President Lee made the comment to those in the room that, "This young man could fill any position in the Church. We should watch him carefully." President Lee also approved the plan the young stake president had put forth.

About twenty years later this same young man, F. David Stanley, was called as a member of the Seventy.

"WITH A VIEW TO WHAT THE MAN MAY BECOME"

President Lee was a visionary, not only in terms of Church organization, but also with regard to the men and women who he served. I was present over a period of many months as President Lee discussed the calling of a new president of Brigham Young University in 1971. After the resignation of long-time president Ernest Wilkinson, a comprehensive search was undertaken to find a qualified replacement. There were many men of great capacity, experience, and stature who were carefully considered as possible candidates, and a large number of well-qualified educators and administrators were interviewed by the Prophet and others.

Among the names to surface in this long process was twenty-nine-year-old Dallin H. Oaks, who was then a law professor at the University of Chicago Law School. To the surprise of many, this unknown young man was chosen to be interviewed along with a slate of prominent candidates.

I was present when Brother Oaks came in to be interviewed. Following the meeting, after

Brother Oaks had left the room, President Lee turned to those present and made this significant, and what I believe to be a prophetic, statement. He commented that resumes and curricula vitae of most of the other candidates greatly excelled that of Brother Oaks, but that "the decision of who to select should not be based upon considerations of what the man now is, but with a view to what the man *may become.*"

Brother Oaks, of course, was selected to lead Brigham Young University, where he served with extraordinary distinction, and he was later called at a relatively young age to the Quorum of the Twelve Apostles.

"THE MOST IMPORTANT MOMENT OF HIS LIFE"

There was a great feeling of love and unity manifested by President Harold B. Lee and the other leading Brethren of the Church on the occasion of his ordination as the eleventh President of the Church on July 7, 1972. I heard several of the Brethren mention on that day the feeling they had that President Lee had been prepared from the foundations of the world for the position of President of the Church.

President Lee was deeply moved after his ordination and showed great emotion, but immediately got hold of himself. He said it was no time for tears. He said that at the most important moment of his life he had no preachment. On several occasions after his ordination, he spoke of a special moment of spiritual enlightenment when it was revealed to him that the entire Church was like a great family, and that each member of this family must be honored and nurtured and loved as family members.

From the moment of his ordination, President Lee spoke like a Prophet. The mantle had truly fallen upon him. He reminded me of President Brigham Young or of one of the Old Testament prophets. He was indeed a Prophet of the living God. He was a man of great capacity. He was a man of deep spiritual insight. I loved him and still love him and am forever grateful to have been blessed to be brought into close contact with him.

"A MASTER AT PRIESTHOOD LEADERSHIP AND DELEGATION"

President Thomas S. Monson once told me that in his opinion, Harold B. Lee was "the greatest delegator in the Church." He was not alone in this opinion. President Lee was a master at priesthood leadership and delegation. He seldom, if ever, did anything himself that he could get someone else to do. He did this not out of a sense of laziness, but with the knowledge that delegation is how future leaders are trained. This also freed him up to focus upon the duties that only he could perform.

President Lee was very fond of telling this story, which illustrates the principle of delegation: He once visited a special multi-stake conference with one of the senior Apostles. The first meeting of the conference was a leadership meeting for the stake presidencies and bishoprics of the stakes involved. To the great surprise of President Lee and the other Apostle, one of the stake presidents was not in attendance. The two counselors in the stake presidency were there, but not the president. After the meeting,

President Lee and the other senior Apostle decided to go to the stake president's home to inquire why he had not attended. They knocked on the man's front door. His wife answered. The Apostles introduced themselves and asked if her husband were home. She replied that he was not, that he had gone to the stake center to help set up chairs for the general meeting. As they left the home, the senior Apostle turned to President Lee and said, "Well, if we have a stake president who insists on doing the work of a deacon, perhaps we should release him and call someone who will fill the role of a stake president."

President Lee never stepped out of his sacred leadership role. I saw him at close hand in two capacities—as a counselor to President Joseph Fielding Smith, and then as President of the Church in his own right. In both capacities he led out with great confidence and firmness, but also with great love. No one ever wondered who was in charge with President Lee at the helm. He was constantly building those around him by giving broad delegations of authority, coupled with a system of making a record of those delegations for follow-through purposes. When

President Lee delegated something, you were always anxious to report to him.

I have mentioned that President Packer once told me that he always felt like a player around his coach when he was in President Lee's presence. I felt the same way, and I know that many others did likewise. There was something about President Lee's leadership style and personality—some special intangible quality or special essence—which made you know that you were in the presence of a master spirit, one of God's elect leaders.

"HIS DAUGHTER APPEARED IN THE SEALING ROOM"

Both during the time he served in the Quorum of the Twelve and later as he served in the First Presidency, President Lee was often called upon to perform marriages for young couples in the Salt Lake Temple. One of these couples was our oldest daughter, Suzanne, and her husband, Timothy Burton, who were sealed by President Lee in 1971. During a single week it was not unusual for him to perform ten or twenty marriages. Most of these marriages were performed in the large sealing rooms on the fourth floor of the temple, but he often liked to use a small sealing room located on the east side of the Salt Lake Temple so that he could walk to the temple from his office in the Church Administration Building. He had a key to one of the huge east doors to the temple so that he could slip in and out quickly.

There were many special spiritual experiences that took place during sealing ceremonies performed by the Prophet. Brother Derek Metcalf, who for many years was engaged in temple work for the Church, one day told me that he was on the fourth floor of the temple sorting through some documents when President Lee walked by and stopped to visit with him. President Lee told Derek that he had just performed the sealing for one of his grandsons, who was the son of his deceased daughter, Maurine Wilkins. President Lee, with some emotion, told Derek that during the ceremony his daughter appeared in the sealing room and stood off to the side observing the sealing of her son to his new bride.

"You Cannot Love the Lord unless You Serve His People"

President Harold B. Lee had a special feeling for the temple. In 1956 he was assigned by the First Presidency to oversee many of the details related to the final construction and then the dedication of the Los Angeles Temple, the largest temple in the Church after the great Salt Lake Temple. One night just prior to the dedication services, President Lee apparently had a powerful spiritual experience, which impacted his future life greatly. On at least three occasions I heard President Lee speak about this special spiritual experience.

The first occasion was in 1970, when I had a long private conversation with President Lee in his office. His office was on the first floor of the Church Administration Building. It was a place of order and peace, with many books on the shelves and pictures and memorabilia hanging on the walls. Prominent among the pictures in his office was a very striking painting of the Savior. As I have mentioned, this picture was given to President Lee by Elder Samuel O. Bennion, a former member of the First Council of the Seventy, shortly before Elder Bennion's death. We sat and talked for an hour or more about a variety of gospel and Church-related subjects. It was one of the most inspiring hours of my life. The conversation turned to personal spiritual experiences. President Lee was very sensitive spiritually, more so than any other man I have known. He was a man who had spiritual experiences and who acted upon them, and through him the Lord manifested His great power.

During this long conversation in his office, President Lee told me that while attending the dedication of the Los Angeles Temple, he had a vivid, moving dream in the nighttime. In his dream he saw President McKay, who stood at a pulpit in a great meeting, and the aged Prophet, with great emphasis and emotion, said to the congregation, "You do not and you cannot love the Lord unless you serve his people and the Church with full purpose of heart!" At the same time in President Lee's dream, there was a great outpouring of the Spirit in the congregation where the Prophet was preaching. President Lee told me that he saw men and women arise in the vast congregation and speak in tongues. He then told me that he saw other things in his dream which he could not relate to me, but he did tell me that because of the things which he saw, he could attest to the close resemblance between the picture of the Savior he had hanging on the wall of his office and the actual appearance of the Savior.

President Lee then told me that a day or two following this powerful dream, during the actual dedication of the Los Angeles Temple, President McKay was the final speaker at the dedicatory services. He told me that the Prophet's appearance and the words of his sermon were so similar to his dream that he was almost overcome with emotion.

I heard him speak about this special dream on two other occasions. First, he mentioned it a few months after our long conversation while speaking to a small group of brethren and sisters, including Sister Gibbons and me. And finally, he alluded to this dream in his concluding address at the end of the April 1973 general conference, when he bore a very moving testimony. As he had before, he retold the vivid dream he had in Los Angeles. I have never before seen the President as touched emotionally as he was after he finished this talk. He sat with his head leaned back against his chair all during the closing prayer with his glasses off and with tears streaming down his face. It was a rare spiritual experience.

"A FREE INTERCHANGE OF IDEAS"

President Harold B. Lee was, in my opinion, an organizational genius of the first magnitude. He was also a gifted leader of men and women and had the ability to bring out the best in everyone around him. From the very first day of my acquaintance with him, I watched him lift those around him to the highest level of creativity and accomplishment. There was always a free interchange of ideas and concepts in his conversation. He would often devote time discussing principles, organization, policies, and personalities with me and with many others. He often shared special spiritual insights and ideas with those around him.

He would also often ask people to prepare memoranda on a variety of subjects we had discussed. He once asked me to write down my recommendations for improving the organization of the missionary work in the Church. I agreed, and President Lee gave me copies of similar written proposals, which he had received from several others, including President Gordon B. Hinckley. This was one of his favorite leadership tools—to foster the freest kind of interchange of ideas and to glean the benefit of the thinking of many people before reaching a final decision dictated by the Spirit.

"Where would the Savior appear?"

President Harold B. Lee took a great interest in the preparation and spiritual training of newly called missionaries. In those days missionaries did not go directly to a Missionary Training Center, but instead would report to what was called the "Mission Home" in Salt Lake City. There, for two weeks or so, they received training from the missionary department staff and the General Authorities of the Church before going on to their fields of labor or to study their mission languages.

President Lee for many years spoke to each group of departing missionaries in the great fifth floor assembly room of the Salt Lake Temple, with its richly carved pulpits facing both east and west. This special meeting occurred after the missionaries had participated in an endowment ceremony in the ordinance rooms below. Following his instruction, President Lee always asked the missionaries if they had any questions, which they invariably did. He would then carefully answer each question, and he was unusually free in his answers, given the sacred setting.

This was a powerful experience for all who participated, and one that I was privileged to witness on several occasions with President Lee. The missionaries all came dressed in white, with their minds focused upon spiritual things, and to then cap off this experience with personal instruction from President Lee, one of the Lord's Apostles, was truly life-changing for the young men and women.

On one occasion President Lee was addressing a large group of missionaries, as usual, when a missionary asked him this question: "Where would the Savior appear if He were to come to this temple?" President Lee considered this question, and then said that since it was the Lord's house, he might appear in any of the rooms of the temple, or even in its hallways. He then said that since the Lord had such a particular interest in missionary work, He most likely would come to the room in which they were then seated because it was used so often for missionary gatherings. At that moment, there was a great emotional outpouring in the room, with many of the young missionaries being moved to tears. President Lee was also moved to tears standing at the pulpit in the assembly room. Finally, without saying a word, he took his seat, where he remained for several minutes. Meanwhile, all was silent in the room, with the young missionaries basking in the spiritual outpouring they were then feeling. Finally, President Lee stood back up and returned to the pulpit. He told the young missionaries that he felt the occasion was too sacred to continue the meeting, but that he wanted them to know that the Savior had been with them that day.

"President Lee wrote a very gentle and thoughtful letter"

One of President Lee's great gifts was the ability to "compose" difficulties. President Gordon B. Hinckley often spoke of learning this principle from President Lee. In the heat of the battle it is best to strive to "compose" disputes rather than to fight them on the field of battle. So, for example, when the Church's attorneys might recommend legal action to assert this or that claim, President Lee's first response was to ask whether it might be best to find a way to "compose" the situation.

This attribute of President Lee met a stern test one day when he received a very brusque and abrasive letter from a woman who deplored the fact that there were not more intellectuals in the local and general leadership of the Church. In his typical way, President Lee wrote the woman a very gentle and thoughtful letter.

A few days later, he received a second letter from this woman. Her tone was very repentant and respectful. She wrote that a few days after mailing her first letter she had fallen and broken her leg. In this she saw divine retribution for what she called her "irascible and intemperate letter" to the Prophet.

"A song about President Lee"

President Howard W. Hunter told me this amusing story not long after President Lee's ordination. It was reported to President Hunter that a young child came home from Primary and with great excitement told his mother that the children had been singing a song about President Lee at the beginning of each Primary opening exercises. When the mother asked the child what the song was, the child began singing, "Reverent-Lee, Quiet-Lee."

President Hunter shared this story with President Lee, who was delighted by it.

"CHURCH LEADERS SHOULD PREACH OPTIMISM, NOT PESSIMISM"

President Harold B. Lee was a man of great optimism. I was once with him in a meeting where several local and general Church leaders were giving presentations. One of the men present began to express his deep pessimism and gloom about the economic future of the United States. President Lee stood up at the conclusion of this brother's presentation and spoke to all present. He did not refer to this brother by name or directly speak about the economic future of the United States, but he remonstrated quite clearly with the tone of the brother's speech. He said that the leaders of the Church have the capacity through their ministry to strongly influence the spirit and tone of our people and of our nation. He then said that Church leaders should preach optimism, not pessimism. He said that those in positions of influence in the Church must look for the strengths and not the weaknesses of the United States and to speak with one voice in building up our nation.

"HE TESTIFIED OF THE PRESENCE OF SPIRITS FROM BEYOND THE VEIL"

We have had few teachers in the Church who were as powerful as Harold B. Lee. I have never heard his equal in the pulpit, before or since. In his preaching, he often brought entire congregations to tears, so powerful was the Spirit that his words invoked. On one occasion when speaking to a group of stake presidencies and bishoprics, his talk seemed more in the nature of a prayer to the Lord than a sermon. He invoked the blessing of the Lord upon those in attendance and prayed that the Holy Ghost would bear witness to them during the meeting. He testified of the presence of the spirits from beyond the veil, and implored God, if it were in His wisdom, that they would manifest themselves to the brethren assembled in the room. After this meeting, President Lee confided that the Lord had taken complete control of him during his remarks in a manner that he had never before experienced, and so he could not claim any credit for anything that he said.

"THEY UNDERSTOOD EVEN BEFORE THE INTERPRETER SPOKE"

In a private conversation in President Lee's home, he shared with my wife, Helen, and me this significant story: He told us of touring the mission and branches of the Church in South America while serving in the Quorum of the Twelve. He had been speaking to a large congregation through an interpreter when he began to notice that many of the saints were nodding assent to what he said before the interpreter finished. During the meeting, a great outpouring of the Spirit occurred, and many, including the interpreter, were overcome with emotion. After the meeting, several of the saints came to him to say that they understood even before the interpreter spoke.

"Experiences Too Sacred to Discuss"

One of my duties as the secretary to the First Presidency was to be the clerk of the General Conferences of the Church. In this capacity, I was privy to all of the preparations that went on behind the scenes, and I sat at a special clerk's desk during each conference session. I can verify that President Harold B. Lee delivered most of his General Conference addresses extemporaneously or only with very simple notes.

This was doubly true with his sermons outside of General Conference. To my knowledge he never wrote out a verbatim sermon, either for General Conference or otherwise. It was contrary to his nature. He was much more effective and uplifting when he spoke extemporaneously. Restricting him to a written talk would have been like caging an eagle. When he could range freely in his thoughts during the sermon, he evoked great spiritual power.

Many of his sermons occupied an hour or more. I recall particularly one sermon he delivered to a large group of Church leaders, which lasted an hour and a half. And yet those that heard him were so doctrinally fed and so spiritually uplifted that it seemed like the briefest of sermons. He concluded this sermon, as with many others, with a very powerful testimony to the effect that he knew with all of his soul that the Church was of divine origin. He testified that he knew this based upon the operation of the Holy Ghost and "experiences too sacred to discuss."

"HE TWICE FELT HANDS PLACED UPON HIS HEAD"

In the last years of his life, President Lee appeared outwardly healthy, but privately was struggling with some serious health issues. Not long before he died, President Lee shared with me this special experience: Some time previously, as he traveled to Salt Lake City from the East Coast, he twice felt hands placed upon his head. Each time he turned and saw no one behind him. However, he felt a powerful manifestation of the Spirit each time and knew that some instrumentality from the unseen world was giving him a blessing to preserve his life. Shortly after he returned home, he was hospitalized. His physician told him that he had a very grave internal ailment. His condition was so serious, the doctor said, that had it erupted in flight, he would almost surely have died.

"HE DIDN'T LOOK ONCE AT THE COLORS"

President Lee's wife, Fern Tanner Lee, died in 1962. The Lees had been married for thirty-nine years. Her passing marked perhaps the greatest trial of President Lee's life.

President Boyd K. Packer told me this touching story from this period in the Prophet's life. When Sister Lee passed away, President Lee could hardly be reconciled. He told the Brethren that he wouldn't attend meetings, and he seemed to have lost all desire to do his work. President Packer told me that President Lee had no hobby to break the tension of his everyday work. He was assigned to go on a mission tour in Europe, which revived him temporarily, but he soon slipped back into a darkness. Then he traveled to a conference on the East Coast. President Packer said that Bill and Ally Marriott took President Lee for a drive to see the beautiful autumn colors in New England. When they returned Ally told Bill, "We might as well not have gone. He didn't look once at the colors."

"I KNOW WHO YOUR HUSBAND WILL BE"

President Lee married his second wife, Joan Jensen Lee, in 1963, more than a year after the death of his first wife, Fern Tanner Lee. As previously mentioned, President Lee had first met Joan Jensen after his mission to Colorado, as Joan was dating one of his former missionary companions at the time. President Lee went on to court and marry Fern Tanner, while Joan Jensen ultimately broke things off with his missionary companion and remained single down through the years.

Sister Joan Lee was a gracious and thoughtful lady, who brightened the life of President Lee following the death of his first wife and through his last years. She was also a woman of great achievement in her own right.

One of the sweetest experiences of my life and the life of my wife, Helen, occurred in the fall of 1970, when we had a long intimate visit with President and Sister Lee in their home in Federal Heights. On a Sunday evening, Sister Joan Lee spoke at a special fireside in the

Bonneville Stake, where Helen and I lived with our family. After the fireside, Helen and I drove Sister Lee home. When we arrived, President Lee came out and invited us inside for a visit. We spent a very memorable hour with them.

As we visited, President Lee turned to his wife and said, "Joan, why don't you tell them about our marriage." Sister Lee then related this inspirational story:

Sister Joan Jensen Lee had remained single until she was sixty-five years old. She was a woman of great ability and great faith and knew that married or single the Lord had a great purpose for her. Many years before, she had received a blessing from President Edward J. Wood in Canada who promised her that she would attain a position in the Church that was far beyond her capacity to imagine. She told us that shortly before her aged mother died, she told her not to be concerned about the future, but to stay close to the Lord and trust in him and that she would receive every blessing pronounced upon her head. So Sister Joan Jensen lived a life filled with faith that the Lord would lead her down the correct path.

Then, when she turned sixty-four years old, about the time Fern Tanner Lee died, Joan Jensen's life changed dramatically. She became engaged to marry a man. One day, not long after her engagement, she went to the home of one of her dearest friends to tell her the big news.

"Guess what?" She began to tell her friend, "I'm getting married."

Her friend interrupted to say, "And I know who your husband will be!"

Joan asked, "Who?"

The friend answered, "Harold B. Lee!"

Sister Joan Jensen was incredulous at this suggestion. However, a short time later, she did in fact break off her engagement with her fiancé for unrelated reasons.

Then one day, some time after she had broken off with this other man, she walked into her home one day to hear the phone ringing. She told us that she knew within herself that it was Brother Lee calling.

She picked up the phone. "Hello?" she said.

"Hello," she heard. "This is Harold Lee calling."

Elder Lee had called to invite her to take a drive to Provo with him. She accepted.

On the day of the drive, Elder Lee pulled up in her driveway and came to the door. They walked back to the car. He held the door open for her. They drove off, and within only a few blocks he proposed!

After Sister Lee told us this story of their engagement, President Lee told us that they had never before told anyone the inspirational circumstances surrounding their marriage.

For Helen and me visiting with President and Sister Lee in their home was without a doubt one of the mountaintop experiences of our lives!

"THE MAN THE CHURCH CAN LEAST AFFORD TO LOSE"

When he was called to the First Presidency in 1970, President Lee was the picture of good health. He had just turned seventy-one years old, and in a Church renown for its octogenarian and nonagenarian leadership, he was still a very young man indeed. He entered into his leadership in the First Presidency with an unprecedented vigor and energy. But there were ominous signs of the hidden health problems that would end his life less than four years later.

The first signs of trouble appeared in late 1972, only a few months after his ordination as the eleventh President of the Church. He suffered a severe bronchial infection, which continued into early 1973. In retrospect, this infection seems very ominous in light of the Prophet's sudden death for bronchial-related symptoms in December of 1973. In late 1972, he developed a very deep-seated cough, which sounded as if he had pneumonia.

By February of 1973, President Lee's cough was still with him, although he had not missed any work. One morning the President invited me to join his counselor, President Marion G. Romney, and Elder Marvin J. Ashton of the Twelve in giving him a special blessing of healing. Elder Ashton anointed the Prophet and the three of us placed our hands on his head as President Romney sealed the anointing. Afterward President Lee said that he did not know of three men on whose faith he would rather rely at that moment in his life. President N. Eldon Tanner, his first counselor, was out of the city at the time. It was a great honor to place my hands on the Prophet's head and to mingle my faith and fervent, silent prayers for his well-being.

President Lee's illness clung to him throughout February and March. In late March he was admitted to the LDS Hospital for some special tests, where he remained for nearly a week. I remember vividly, on the day of President Lee's release from the hospital, I saw President Boyd K. Packer on the steps of the Administration Building, who inquired about the Prophet's condition. President Packer echoed the general feeling of everyone when he said, "We must pray to God for his recovery. President Lee is the man the Church can least afford to lose!"

After his release from the hospital in early spring of 1973, President Lee began to take special treatment at his home, once in the morning and once at night, to try to clear out his lungs. These continued throughout the spring of 1973.

"THE TWO PROPHETS STOOD UPON MARS HILL AS THE SUN WAS RISING"

In September of 1972, two months after becoming President of the Church, President Lee made an extended trip to Europe in the company of President Gordon B. Hinckley, then a member of the Quorum of the Twelve, and their wives, Joan Jensen Lee and Marjorie Pay Hinckley. Their itinerary took them to London, where they were honored at two dinners hosted by Lord Thompson of Fleet—one with the Bulgarian Ambassador, where the Prophet held private discussions about the possibility of preaching the gospel in Bulgaria, and a second dinner with English religious leaders. The wealthy and influential Lord Thompson, who for many years was one of the great friends of the Church in England, also introduced President Lee to influential people from Israel. From England they traveled to Italy, where President Lee spoke to about 250 recent converts to the Church. The Lees and the Hinckleys then traveled to Greece, where diplomatic attempts were made to obtain special "house of worship status" for the Church, allowing us to finally open Greece for the preaching of the Gospel. From Greece they flew to Israel, where steps were taken to improve the Church's relationships with government officials. Finally, they flew to Bern, Switzerland, where President Lee installed a new temple presidency.

When President Lee returned to Salt Lake City, he shared with me this inspirational story. While in Athens, President Lee and President Hinckley walked together early one morning up Mars Hill with their scriptures. The two Prophets stood upon Mars Hill, amid the ancient ruins, as the sun was rising over the Acropolis and the Parthenon. President Lee then opened his scriptures and read aloud from Acts, Chapter 17:

> Now while Paul waited at Athens, his spirit was stirred in him. . . .
>
> Then Paul stood in the midst of Mars' hill, and said, Ye men of Athens, I perceive that in all things ye are too superstitious.
>
> For as I passed by, and beheld your devotions, I found an altar with this inscription, TO THE UNKNOWN GOD. Whom therefore ye ignorantly worship, him declare I unto you. (Acts 17:16, 22, 23)

"WE HAVE COME TO THE LAND OF MIRACLES"

President Lee's long trip with President Gordon B. Hinckley through Europe and the Middle East took place in September of 1972. This was only two months after the Prophet's ordination as the eleventh President of the Church. This trip was important for the Church in many ways. It greatly strengthened our relationships with friends of the Church in Europe, and it opened the door for the ultimate preaching of the gospel or establishment of the Church in Greece, parts of Eastern Europe, and in Israel. My sense is that it was also very personally significant for both President Lee and President Hinckley.

In about 1982 I had a lengthy conversation with President Hinckley, in which he shared with me these additional insights about this most significant trip.

It was obvious to me from the time I began serving the First Presidency that a strong bond existed between President Lee and President Hinckley. From comments both men made to me, I understand that this bond extended back to the days when they were both staff employees of the Church. Before their calls as General Authorities, President Lee was employed as the Managing Director of the Welfare Department and President Hinckley as the executive secretary of the Radio and Publicity Committee. There are other connections between the two Prophets. It was President Lee who called President Hinckley as a stake president. President Lee later told President Hinckley that when he set him apart, he "saw what was ahead" for him.

Shortly after President Lee was sustained as the President of the Church in July 1972, he went to President Hinckley and asked him to be his traveling companion on a long trip together with their wives, which would take them to Europe and the Holy Land. President Hinckley told me that this was one of the great privileges of his life, to accompany the Prophet in this manner.

President Hinckley said that during the beginning stage of the journey, as the Lees and the Hinckleys visited England, Italy, and Greece, President Lee seemed in perfect health. Then, in Jerusalem, President Lee began having respiratory problems and took ill with heavy congestion in his lungs. The Hinckleys occupied a room adjacent to the

Lees in their hotel in Jerusalem. One night there was a knock on President Hinckley's door. It was Sister Joan Lee, the Prophet's wife. Concerned about her husband, Sister Joan Lee asked President Hinckley to come and administer to the Prophet. President Lee in turn invited President Ted Cannon (who was then serving as the mission president in Switzerland with jurisdiction over Jerusalem and who was traveling with them) to come and assist in giving President Lee a priesthood blessing. Brother Cannon anointed the Prophet, and President Hinckley sealed the anointing, giving him a blessing of health.

Later that night, President Hinckley said he heard loud coughing from President Lee's adjoining room, which continued for some time and then stopped. The next morning at breakfast when the Cannons were present, President Lee said nothing about his health. But the following day, after the Cannons had departed, President Lee said privately to President Hinckley at breakfast, "I guess we have had to come to the land of miracles to see miracles in our own lives." He then explained that some time after receiving the priesthood administration from President Hinckley and Brother Cannon, he had taken a severe spell so serious that he felt he was going to die. Finally, he said, he coughed up a large clot of blood and that the coughing then stopped.

"A REVELATION THAT THE ENTIRE CHURCH WAS A SINGLE FAMILY"

It was a moving experience to observe President Harold B. Lee firsthand in the weeks and months following his ordination as President of the Church in 1972. He had always been a man of great spirituality, but that quality was magnified by the heavy burden that had been laid upon his shoulders. He was transformed in other ways. He now seemed to have taken upon himself a powerful quality of love, kindness, and empathy toward those around him. During his entire presidency he conducted himself as a loving father in the midst of a great family.

I attribute these changes to the special spiritual experience already mentioned, which the Prophet alluded to several times in my presence in 1972. He spoke of this special experience as "a revelation." On the day he was ordained, I heard him say that it had come to him "as a revelation" that the entire church was a single family, and that each member of that family should be loved and nurtured and honored as a family member, each in his or her own place.

"A DREAM IN WHICH HE SAW THREE MEN SITTING AT A TABLE"

President Harold B. Lee, like all of the Presidents who went before him or succeeded him, was sought out by a multitude of people. There was a constant stream of visitors who came to see the Prophet at 47 East South Temple. Among the most memorable was a delegation of Native Americans from the Arapahoe and Cheyenne tribes. They came in the early days of President Lee's administration. There were many members of this delegation, none of whom were members of the Church. They were all received by the Prophet and his counselors and most of the members of the Twelve in the large council room, with President Lee and his counselors sitting at the head of the table. President Lee explained to these visitors that the Church was directed by a First Presidency of three men and a Quorum of Twelve Apostles, and that when a President of the Church passed away, as had President Joseph Fielding Smith, a new Prophet was chosen, ordained, and sustained from among the living Apostles.

Pleasantries were exchanged, and it appeared the meeting was over. Then one of the men spoke up and asked the Prophet if he could share a personal experience. President Lee told him he would be delighted to listen. The man then told President Lee that several months previously he had a vivid dream in which he saw three men sitting at the head of a table. One of the men, seated in the middle, was very aged. He also saw twelve other men seated at an adjacent table, with six on each side. In his dream, he then saw the most elderly of the three men rise to his feet, and give his place to one of the younger men seated by his side. This man then said that he now knew the interpretation of his dream—that it represented the change in the Mormon First Presidency, which had just been explained to him.

President Lee seemed deeply moved by this experience, and even more so when we learned that this Native American man had been taught the gospel and was baptized in the Salt Lake Tabernacle font a short time later.

"Let every man learn and act"

President Harold B. Lee was a builder of men and women. His style of leadership was unusually free and inspiring. His philosophy was to inspire them to the highest level of their capacity, and then get out of their way and let them serve with all their might. He often quoted the scripture in the Doctrine and Covenants 107:99, "Wherefore, now let every man learn his duty, and to act in the office in which he is appointed, in all diligence." He then would add this insight—that it is of utmost important that we "let" every man learn and act. We are too inclined as leaders, he said, to attempt to dictate every action of our people. What the Lord wants, he testified, is for us to "let" or permit every man to learn and then perform his duty. Leaders, he said, must act as coaches and not as players in the game of service.

"HE FELT AN UNSEEN PRESENCE IN THE CIRCLE"

While serving as a counselor in the First Presidency, President Lee shared with me this special spiritual experience, which had occurred years earlier. His memory of this experience was triggered when he drove to Malad, Idaho, in about 1970 to speak at the funeral services for Dr. Thomas Richards. His widow was Hilda Merrill Richards, a daughter of the late Apostle Marriner W. Merrill. President Lee had first become acquainted with Brother and Sister Richards in the late 1940's when Brother Richards served as president of the Central States Mission of the Church.

President Lee recalled to me that he had given a blessing to Brother Richards' wife while he was touring the Central States Mission. Sister Richards was very distraught and despondent over the sudden death of one of their children. President Lee told me that as he and President Richards laid their hands on the head of Sister Hilda Richards, he felt an unseen presence in the circle and he knew it to be her father, Elder Marriner W. Merrill.

After the blessing, President Richards told President Lee that he felt the same thing.

"PRESIDENT LEE COULD BE LIKENED TO THE ARCHITECT"

Because of the brevity of his service in the prophetic office, President Lee is little remembered today by the membership of the Church. He served only eighteen months as the President of the Church, from July of 1972 until his unexpected death in December of 1973. But his minor renown is in no way indicative of his true legacy.

President Lee was a man of extraordinary vision and leadership ability, who laid the groundwork of many concepts and initiatives that President Spencer W. Kimball saw to full implementation. Among these initiatives were the opening of new doors to the preaching of the gospel, the expansion of temple work, the reorganization of Church administration at headquarters, and the holding of area conferences and solemn assemblies around the world. In many ways President Kimball acted as the "Joshua" to President Harold B. Lee's "Moses." Or, to look at it in another light, President Lee could be likened to the architect who constructed a powerful machine, and President Kimball could be likened to a superior driver who moved the vehicle forward.

"The Man to Lead God's People"

President Lee received a credible death threat in about August of 1973. The day after the threat was received, I had a long visit with the Prophet in his office. I made the comment to President Lee that he was probably experiencing some of the tension and uncertainty that was the Prophet Joseph Smith's portion during most of his adult life. This elicited a ready response from President Lee. He observed to me that this episode might be the means of further disciplining and training him. He then read to me an excerpt from a General Conference sermon delivered in the Tabernacle in 1853 by Elder Orson Hyde, reported in the *Journal of Discourses*. The sermon is entitled, "The Man to Lead God's People." It describes the process through which a man must go in order to prepare him for the prophetic office. Here is the excerpt President Lee referred to:

> It is generally the case, and I think I may say it is invariably the case, that when an individual is ordained and appointed to lead the people, he has passed through tribulations and trials,

and has proven himself before God, and before His people, that he is worthy of the situation which he holds. And let this be the motto and safeguard in all future time, that when a person that has not been tried, that has not proved himself before God, and before His people, and before the councils of the Most High, to be worthy, he is not going to step in to lead the Church and people of God. It never has been so, but from the beginning some one that understands the Spirit and counsel of the Almighty, that knows the Church, and is known of her, is the character that will lead the Church.

How does he become thus acquainted? How does he gain this influence, this confidence in the estimation of the people? He earns it by his upright course and conduct, by the justness of his counsels, and the correctness of his prophecies, and the straightforward spirit he manifests to the people. And he has to do this step by step; he gains influence, and his spirit, like an anchor, is fastened in the hearts of the people; and he is sustained and supported by the love, confidence, and good-will of the Saints, and of Him that dwelt in the bush. This is the kind of character that ought to lead God's people, after he has obtained this good will and this confidence. (Journal of Discourses, vol. 1, p. 123)

President Lee told me that in reading this sermon he almost felt as if he were reading his own biography. He commented on some of the disappointments and difficulties he had encountered during the more than thirty years he had served as a General Authority.

About a week later, with this death threat still on his mind, President Lee again visited privately with me. He again alluded to the many difficulties he had been called upon to endure since being called to Quorum of the Twelve. He then said that he would not have been prepared to lead were it not for "the edifying effect of those experiences."

"Foxes have holes and birds have nests"

In October of 1973 a second, and much more serious threat was made against President Lee's life. In the aftermath of this threat, the Prophet was very calm and seemed to have no real fear or concern. An indication of how lonely the President must have felt at this critical time was this statement that he made. He told me, "I now have a little better understanding of the Master's statement, 'Foxes have holes and birds have nests, but the Son of Man has nowhere to lay his head.'"

"One Final Conversation with President Lee"

As Christmas approached in 1973, I had no inkling of the vast changes in the Church that would occur in the space of a few days. I worked in the offices of the First Presidency as usual through Friday, December 21, 1973. At the end of the workday I went to wish President Lee a happy holiday season. He invited me into his office, and then said to me, in substance, "Brother Gibbons, in the language of scripture, I look upon you as a friend and in no sense as a subordinate or servant." When I expressed thanks for my association with him, he answered, "Brother Gibbons, there is no one with whom I feel a closer kinship of spirit than you."

I didn't realize it at the time, but this was the last face-to-face conversation I would have with the Prophet in this lifetime.

I did, however, have one final conversation with President Lee by telephone. Late in the evening on Christmas Day, I received a phone call from President Lee. Among other things, he said to me, "Brother Gibbons, I just wanted to take this opportunity to wish you and yours a Merry Christmas. I had intended," he said, "to come to your house today to pay you a visit, but you can't imagine the turmoil we have had here." He continued, "We did go over to Helen's and Brent's." Then he added, "I have little gifts for you, President Tanner, and President Romney. Since I won't be at the office tomorrow, I will send your gift down there for you." He then expressed appreciation for my service and mentioned the confidence he had in me. He then asked if we had a good Christmas. In answering, I mentioned the fact that we had all been together, including our first grandson. He said, "Is that the child of our special girl?" meaning our daughter Suzanne. When I said, "Yes," President Lee commented on the special circumstances surrounding her birth, which I have previously described.

This phone conversation was the last one I had with this great Prophet. The following day, December 26, 1973, he died at about 9:00 p.m. He had gone to the LDS Hospital in Salt Lake City for his annual check-up. While in the hospital, he apparently experienced some of the same kind of congestion that bothered him so much during the last year of his life. His personal secretary, Brother Arthur

Haycock, who called me immediately afterward, was with the Prophet at the time of his death. He said that the President had a mask over his face to help him breathe, when he suddenly seemed to be in distress. A glassy look came into his eyes, and he seemed ready to faint. Arthur summoned a nurse and doctor, but it was to no avail. He was gone with a few minutes of "lung and heart arrest."

Only God knows how much I loved this great man and how much I miss him. God bless his memory.

"No righteous man dies before his time"

President Harold B. Lee's funeral was held on Friday, December 28, 1973. The Prophet's body lay in state from 8:00 a.m. to 8:00 p.m. in the foyer of the Administration Building. More than ten thousand people came to pay their respects and view his remains, passing solemnly through the marble foyer. Several of the Prophet's stalwart grandsons were present all during this time, standing beside the casket.

It was a wet and dreary day on which to lay President Lee in the cold ground. The funeral cortege left the Administration Building about 11:30 a.m., following the family prayer. The funeral was held in the Tabernacle. The speakers were President Spencer W. Kimball, future Church President Gordon B. Hinckley, and the two men who served as counselors to Presidents Lee and Kimball, Presidents N. Eldon Tanner and Marion G. Romney.

I recall that President Tanner was highly emotional during his funeral sermon and at times could hardly speak. President Kimball was greatly magnified, and it was evident as he spoke that the prophetic mantle had already fallen upon him.

I was most struck and comforted by something President Gordon B. Hinckley said in his funeral sermon. He said of President Harold B. Lee, "No righteous man dies before his time."

About the Author

Daniel Bay Gibbons is a writer living in Holladay, Utah. The youngest son of Francis M. Gibbons and Helen Bay Gibbons, he is a former trial attorney and judge and is the author of several previous books. He has served as a full-time missionary, twice as a bishop, and as president of the Russia Novosibirsk Mission.

INDEX

Acropolis, 96
Albion State
  Normal School, 5
Albion State
  School, 17
Arapahoe, 102
Area Conferences
  Manchester, 10
  Mexico City, 10
  Munich, 10
Ashton, Elder
  Marvin J., 93
Bennion, Elder
  Samuel O., 42,
  69
Benson, President
  Ezra Taft
  boyhood
    friendship with
    HBL, 16
  service in the
    Twelve, 36
Bern, Switzerland,
  96
Bonneville Stake,
  89
Brigham Young
  University, 61
Bulgaria, 95
Burton, Elder
  Theodore M., 32
Burton, Suzanne
  Gibbons, 56, 67
Burton, Timothy A.,
  57, 67
Cache Valley, 13,
  17, 22
Callis, Elder
  Charles A., 8
  death of, 8, 44
  vision of the
    Savior, 43
Cannon, Ted, 99
Cheyenne, 102
Chicago Law
  School, 60
Church
  Administration
  Building, 27, 67

City Creek Canyon, 34
Clark
  President J. Reuben and HBL, 38
Clark, President J. Reuben, 7, 40, 41
  and HBL, 36, 49
  prophecy of, 7, 48
Clawson, President Rudger, 27
Clifton Ward, 18
Clifton, Idaho, 13, 15
Cowley, Elder Matthew, 36
Death Valley, 50
Denver, Colorado, 19
England, 95
Ensign Stake, 6
Federal Heights, 88
First Council of the Seventy, 42
First Presidency, 7

Gibbons, Francis M.
  first acquaintance with HBL, 52
  last conversation with HBL, 113
Gibbons, Helen Bay, 71
  blessing from HBL, 53
Grant, President Heber J., 6, 7, 23, 33, 35
Great Depression, 30
Greece, 95
Haycock, Arthur, 114
Hinckley, Marjorie Pay, 95
Hinckley, President Gordon B., 78, 116
  and HBL, 73, 95
  travels with HBL, 10

with HBL in
Israel, 97
Hunter, President
Howard W., 13
and HBL, 80
Hyde, Elder Orson,
109
Italy, 95
Jacksonville,
Florida, 8, 44
Jensen, Harriet
prophecy of, 19
Jerusalem, 99
Kimball, President
Spencer W., 48,
116
and legacy of
HBL, 107
service in the
Twelve, 36
Knight, John M.,
20, 22
Latin America, 58
LDS Hospital, 93
Lee, Fern Tanner,
6, 22, 25
death of, 9, 87

Lee, Joan Jensen,
9, 22, 95
courtship of with
HBL, 88
Lee, Louisa, 13
Lee, Louisa
Bingham, 5
Lee, President
Harold B.
ancestry, 13
and dream of
Native
American
leader, 103
and GBH, 97
and picture of the
Savior, 42
and the Temple,
69
and the Welfare
Program, 26,
30, 32, 33
and Welfare
Program, 38
blessing to Helen
Bay Gibbons,
53

boyhood friendship with ETB, 16
conducts funeral for Charles A. Callis, 45
courtship with Joan Jensen, 89
dreams of, 29, 50, 70
experience in Los Angeles Temple, 69
extemporaneous Conference sermons, 84
gift of tongues, 83
home of, 88
legacy, 107
life
  and the Welfare Program, 7
  Apostolic service, 7, 36, 41
  birth, 5
  call to the Twelve, 35, 39, 44, 48
  childhood, 13
  Church service, 6, 18, 25
  counselor to JFS, 9
  death, 11
  death of, 113
  death threats, 109, 112
  education, 5, 16
  employment, 25
  funeral of, 116
  health problems, 92, 98
  marriage to Fern Tanner, 6, 25
  marriage to Joan Jensen Lee, 9
  miraculous healing in

    Jerusalem, 10
    mission, 5, 19, 20
    political career, 6, 7, 26, 33
    President of the Church, 10, 62, 101, 102
    travels, 8, 9, 10, 95, 97
    work, 5
    writing, 8
  musical talent, 13
  office of, 69
  personal
    qualities, 13
    administration, 64, 104
    eloquence, 75
    faith, 99
    mentor, 58
    optimism, 81
    organizational genius, 73
    pesuasion, 78
    sense of humor, 80
    spirituality, 15, 19, 24, 27, 33, 68, 72, 82, 83, 86, 105
    spirituality, 8
    vision, 31
  receives blessing Jerusalem from GBH, 99
Lee, Samuel Marion, Jr., 5
Lord Thompson of Fleet, 95
Los Angeles Temple dedication of, 69
Malad, Idaho, 105
Manchester, England, 10
Marriott, Ally, 87
Marriott, Bill, 87
Mars Hill
  HBL preaches on, 96
McConkie, Oscar W., Jr.,, 50

McConkie, Oscar W., Sr.
  dream of, 50
McKay, President David O., 7
  death of, 9
Meeks, Heber, 44
Merrill, Elder Marriner W., 105
Metcalf, Derek, 67
Mexico, 8
Mexico City, 10
Miami, Florida, 44
Mission Home, 75
Missionary Training Center, 75
Monson, President Thomas S.
  and HBL, 64
Moyle, President Henry D., 36
Munich, Germany, 10
Native Americans, 102
New York City, 9
Oaks, Elder Dallin H.
  and HBL, 60
Oneida Stake Academy, 16
Oxford, Idaho, 5, 18
Packer, President Boyd K., 87, 93
  and HBL, 40
Palo Alto, California, 53
Parthenon, 96
Patriarch to the Church, 41
Petersen, Elder Mark E., 36
Pioneer Stake, 6, 7, 25, 27, 30, 32, 33, 58
Poplar Grove Ward, 25
Preston, Idaho, 16
Quorum of the Twelve, 35
Radio and Publicity Committee, 98
Richards, Dr. Thomas, 105

Richards, Hilda Merrill
  blessed by HBL, 105
Richards, President Stephen L., 46
Romney, President Marion G., 36, 93, 116
Safford, Arizona, 7, 48
Salt Lake City Commission, 6, 26
Salt Lake Tabernacle, 103
Salt Lake Temple, 6, 9, 42, 57, 67, 69
  missionary training in, 75
Seventy, 59
Smith, Elder Nicholas G., 41
Smith, President George Albert, 27
Smith, President Joseph, 109
Smith, President Joseph Fielding, 9, 38, 65, 102
  death of, 10
South Africa Mission, 9
South America, 9
Stanford University, 52
Stanley, Elder F. David
  and HBL, 59
Stapley, Elder Delbert L., 36
Switzerland, 99
Talmage, Elder James E., 22
  corrects young HBL, 20
Tanner, President N. Eldon, 93, 116
Van Valkenburg, Mac, 55
Welfare Program, 7, 26, 38
Western States Mission, 5, 24

Weston, Idaho, 5, 17
Whitney, Elder Orson F.
 vision of the Savior, 42
Whittier Elementary School, 25
Wilkins, Ernie, 53
Wilkins, Maurine Lee, 53
 appearance in Temple, 68
Wilkinson, Ernest, 60
Wood, Edward J.
 gives prophetic blessing to Joan Lee, 89
Young, President Brigham, 63
Youth and the Church book by HBL, 8

www.ingramcontent.com/pod-product-compliance
Lightning Source LLC
Chambersburg PA
CBHW071518080526
44588CB00011B/1473